GUARDED

STUDY GUIDE

For foreign and subsidiary rights, contact the author.

Cover design by: Sara Young
Bio photo by: Tonya Damron
Cover photo by: Meshelle Robbins (The Avenue Church Photography Team)

ISBN: 978-1-962401-51-7   1 2 3 4 5 6 7 8 9 10

Printed in the United States of America

MELISSA GRAHAM

GUARDED

STUDY GUIDE

AVAIL

Contents

HEART CENTRAL

Our whole existence is tied to the health of our hearts: physically, spiritually, and emotionally.

READING TIME

As you read Chapter 1: "Heart Central" in *Guarded*, review, reflect on, and respond to the text by answering the following questions.

REFLECT AND TAKE ACTION:

What does it mean to you personally that the heart is "the epicenter" of your life? How do you see this truth affecting your daily decisions and walk with the Lord?

_____

_____

_____

_____

_____

_____

Reflect on the vital connection between your physical and spiritual heart. What is the significance of this connection for living life with a guarded heart?

_____

_____

_____

_____

_____

_____

What is the relationship between wisdom and a guarded heart?

_____

_____

_____

_____

_____

_____

> *"Today, if you hear His voice, do not harden your hearts."*
> —**Hebrews 3:15 (ESV)**

Consider the scripture above and answer the following questions:

Recall a time when your heart softened to His voice and a time when your heart resisted His voice. To what do you attribute those responses?

_____

_____

_____

_____

_____

Are there particular areas of your life where you tend to resist or ignore God's voice? Why?

_____

_____

_____

_____

_____

Consider a time when poor wisdom opened your heart to things that pulled you away from the heartbeat of Jesus. What was that experience like?

_____

_____

_____

_____

_____

Consider a time when you exercised good wisdom by shielding
your heart from harmful things. What kind of fruit was
produced?

_____

_____

_____

_____

_____

_____

Reflect on the concept that your heart's condition determines
your life's direction. How have you seen this play out in your
own life?

_____

_____

_____

_____

_____

_____

Meditate on the biblical meaning of guarding your heart, laid out in Proverbs 4:23. What exactly are you to guard your heart against?

_____

_____

_____

_____

_____

_____

_____

Are there any areas of your life (e.g., relationships, sin, addictions, etc.) where you are in denial of the reality of your heart's spiritual health? What is preventing you from addressing it?

_____

_____

_____

_____

_____

_____

_____

Consider the statement in Jeremiah 17:4 that says our hearts are the most deceptive and wicked thing of all. In what ways does this truth challenge you? In what ways does it encourage you?

_____

_____

_____

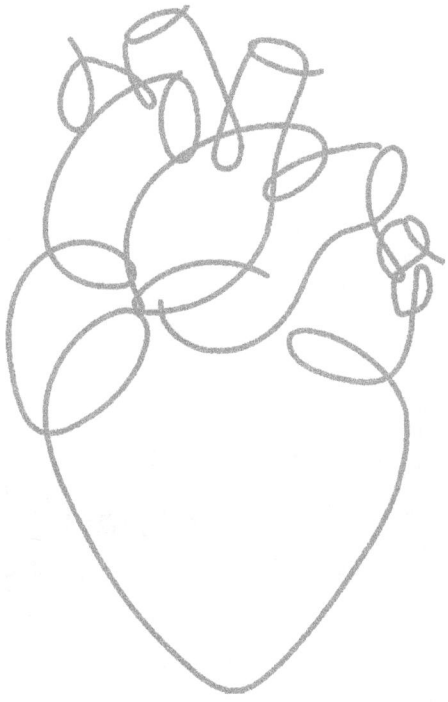

MY HEART, MY RESPONSIBILITY

We all have a heart history, and we need to identify it and address it appropriately.

READING TIME

As you read
Chapter 2:
"My Heart, My
Responsibility"
in *Guarded*,
review,
reflect on,
and respond
to the text by
answering
the following
questions.

REFLECT AND TAKE ACTION:

Reflect on a time when you found it challenging to take responsibility for your actions. How did shifting the blame affect your relationships and your heart?

_____

_____

_____

_____

_____

_____

_____

_____

_____

How does the story of Jocelyn and Judah highlight the importance of teaching responsibility from a young age? How does it apply to your life?

_____

_____

_____

_____

_____

_____

_____

_____

_____

The author emphasizes the need for personal responsibility in guarding your heart. How does this resonate with your experiences in managing your spiritual life?

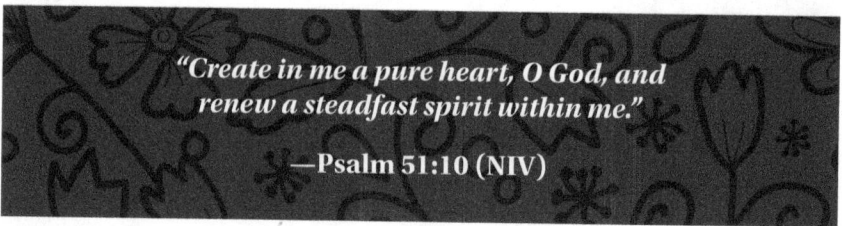

_____

_____

_____

_____

_____

_____

_____

_____

> *"Create in me a pure heart, O God, and renew a steadfast spirit within me."*
>
> **—Psalm 51:10 (NIV)**

Consider the scripture above and answer the following questions:

What areas of your life require renewal? How can this verse guide you in seeking God's help to purify your heart?

_____

_____

_____

_____

_____

_____

_____

How does this scripture influence your understanding of repentance and its relationship to the condition of your heart?

_____

_____

_____

_____

_____

_____

_____

How do you handle the responsibility of guarding your heart in everyday life? What areas need more attention?

_____

_____

_____

_____

_____

_____

Recall a time when you took full responsibility for a negative interaction that exposed the condition of your heart. What did you learn from that experience?

_____

_____

_____

_____

_____

_____

_____

_____

_____

How does the story of sibling interactions in the chapter remind you of the need for grace and accountability in relationships? Is there someone you need to extend grace to today?

_____

_____

_____

_____

_____

_____

_____

_____

_____

Consider the balance between giving and receiving grace in your life. How does this balance (or imbalance) impact your heart's health?

_____

_____

_____

_____

_____

_____

_____

_____

_____

Take a moment to consider your thought life. How is it impacting your emotions, and what recurring thought could you commit to aligning with the Word of God today?

_____

_____

_____

_____

_____

_____

_____

_____

_____

CHAPTER 3

ECHO

You cannot hide what's inside.

READING TIME

As you read Chapter 3: "Chapter Name" in *Book Name*, reflect on, and respond to the text by answering the following questions.

REFLECT AND TAKE ACTION:

How do the concepts of echoes and heart-beats symbolize the ongoing impact of your past experiences on your present life?

_____

_____

_____

_____

_____

_____

_____

_____

_____

_____

What does it mean for your life to be an "echo" of your heart? What kind of echo is your life communicating to the world?

_____

_____

_____

_____

_____

_____

_____

_____

_____

_____

_____

> *"A good man brings good things out of good stored up in his heart."*
>
> —Luke 6:45

Consider the scripture above and answer the following questions:

What "good things" are being produced in your life? What "bad things" are being produced? What does this reveal about what you are storing in your heart daily?

_____

_____

_____

_____

_____

_____

_____

How intentional are you in storing up good things in your heart, such as love, kindness, truth, and good boundaries? How could you become more intentional?

_____

_____

_____

_____

_____

_____

_____

Refer to the echo cycle diagram in this chapter. In your own words, how do the three elements of the cycle (source, sound, symphony) work together to "tell on your heart"?

_____

_____

_____

_____

_____

_____

_____

The author discusses the importance of setting a standard for your life. What standards have you set, how do they align with your spiritual goals, and what you would like to see happen in your relationship with Jesus?

_____

_____

_____

_____

_____

_____

_____

_____

Reflect on the idea of past wounds continuing to echo in your heart. What past wounds have gone unaddressed or are still in the active process of healing? What steps can you begin to take toward healing?

_____

_____

_____

_____

_____

_____

_____

_____

The author states that you cannot hide what's inside of you because what is in you will always come out. How do you respond to that statement? What emotions does this statement trigger, and why?

_____

_____

_____

_____

_____

_____

_____

_____

_____

Take a moment to evaluate the present condition of your echo cycle. Are you pleased with how your cycle is operating? Why or why not? Explain in detail any observations you make regarding the aspects of your cycle that need shaping up.

_____

_____

_____

_____

_____

_____

_____

_____

_____

_____

HEART INVADERS

The root of fear forges deeper into our hearts when our need to control the outcome is more significant than our belief that He's in control.

READING
TIME

As you read
Chapter 4:
"Heart
Invaders"
in *Guarded*,
review,
reflect on,
and respond
to the text by
answering
the following
questions.

REFLECT AND TAKE ACTION:

This chapter discusses the reality of "heart invaders." What invaders have you allowed into your heart, and what observations have you made about their tactics?

_____

_____

_____

_____

_____

_____

_____

_____

_____

Reflect on the process of heart diagnosis described in the chapter. How do you conduct spiritual "check-ups" to address issues in your heart?

_____

_____

_____

_____

_____

_____

_____

_____

_____

_____

How successful have you been in confronting and defeating your invaders? What does God expect us to do when our hearts become vulnerable to invaders?

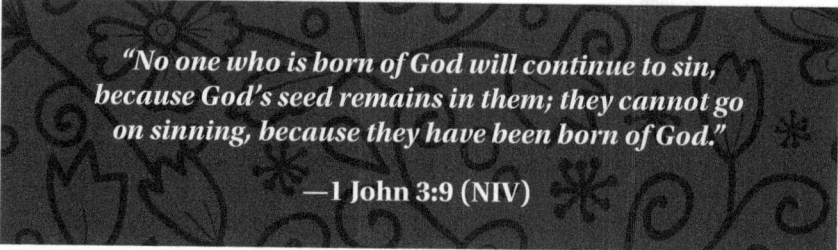

_____

_____

_____

_____

_____

_____

_____

> *"No one who is born of God will continue to sin, because God's seed remains in them; they cannot go on sinning, because they have been born of God."*
>
> —1 John 3:9 (NIV)

Consider the scripture above and answer the following questions:

What is the difference between the kind of sin referred to in this scripture and habitual sin?

_____

_____

_____

_____

_____

_____

_____

What about being born of God as carriers of His seed keeps us from habitual sin? How does our surrender to Christ protect our hearts from it?

_____

_____

_____

_____

_____

_____

_____

The author discusses how belief steers behavior and suggests we challenge every belief in our hearts by working backward (isolate a behavior, investigate the belief behind it, weigh it with God's Word, and respond to its truth). Choose one belief that you need to challenge, follow these steps, and jot down what you discover.

_____

_____

_____

_____

_____

_____

_____

How do you balance openness to others with the need to protect your heart from harmful influences?

_____

_____

_____

_____

_____

_____

_____

_____

_____

What boundaries has God set for you in various areas of your life (physical, emotional, and spiritual)? How well do you keep them? Have you ever suffered the consequences of violating God's boundaries?

_____

_____

_____

_____

_____

_____

_____

_____

_____

Insert yourself in Julia's story. Where can you trace the entrance and activity of heart intruders, and at what points would you respond to proactively develop a guarded heart?

_____

_____

_____

_____

_____

_____

_____

_____

_____

The author identifies seven heart invaders: fear, busyness, unworthiness, unforgiveness, anxiety/depression, apathy, and pride. Which of these invaders shows up most often in your life? What needs to happen to weaken their power over your heart?

_____

_____

_____

_____

_____

_____

_____

_____

CHAPTER 5

HEART ON FIRE

If the stronghold of control remains in your heart, you are in danger of thinking your ideas are God's ideas.

REFLECT AND TAKE ACTION:

How would you explain God as Fire in your own words?

_____

_____

_____

_____

_____

_____

_____

_____

_____

_____

How does understanding the concept of a controlled burn help you see the value in God allowing challenges in your life to refine you? What areas of your life are in need of a controlled burn?

_____

_____

_____

_____

_____

_____

_____

_____

_____

_____

Refer to the list of things we can do to make sure the atmosphere of our hearts will burn the way God desires. Which of these stands out to you the most, and why?

_____

_____

_____

_____

_____

_____

_____

_____

> "This means that anyone who belongs to Christ has become a new person. The old life is gone; a new life has begun!"
>
> —1 Corinthians 5:17 (NLT)

Consider the scripture above and answer the following questions:

What specific areas of your life reflect the newness of life that Christ has brought? How do you continue to cultivate this new life daily?

_____

_____

_____

_____

_____

_____

_____

Reflect on an aspect of your old life that you have struggled to leave behind. How does this scripture encourage you to fully embrace the new life Christ offers?

_____

_____

_____

_____

_____

_____

Meditate on this statement about the atmosphere of our lives: "When we choose to take steps to change it, God is faithful in meeting us in the middle." What steps have you taken to change the atmosphere of your life? What steps can you commit to taking now?

_____

_____

_____

_____

_____

_____

_____

Identify the place in your life in need of an atmosphere adjustment. What needs to happen to follow God's prescription for your heart?

_____

_____

_____

_____

_____

_____

_____

_____

Describe a time when you recognized that God had been working on your behalf even when you had taken the wrong path. What did you learn about who God is in your failure?

_____

_____

_____

_____

_____

_____

_____

_____

Who in your life are you accountable to? How do you respond to accountability, and where might you need more of it?

_____

_____

_____

_____

_____

_____

_____

_____

Reflect on a time when your passion for God diminished. What caused it, and how did you rekindle that fire?

_____

_____

_____

_____

_____

_____

_____

_____

What practical steps can you take daily to intentionally tend to the flame of your heart?

_____

_____

_____

_____

_____

_____

_____

Guarded to Gain

*It costs us nothing to be loved by God but
everything to be trusted by Him.*

READING TIME

As you read Chapter 6: "Guarded to Gain" in *Guarded*, review, reflect on, and respond to the text by answering the following questions.

REFLECT AND TAKE ACTION:

The author's story of her daughter's academic success illustrates the importance of guarding and nurturing the gifts God has given us. What gifts or talents in your life require more intentional guarding?

_____

_____

_____

_____

_____

_____

_____

_____

_____

How does the principle that "if we don't stop gaining, He won't stop giving" resonate with your own experience?

_____

_____

_____

_____

_____

_____

_____

_____

_____

_____

What small thing has God entrusted you with, and what are you doing with it?

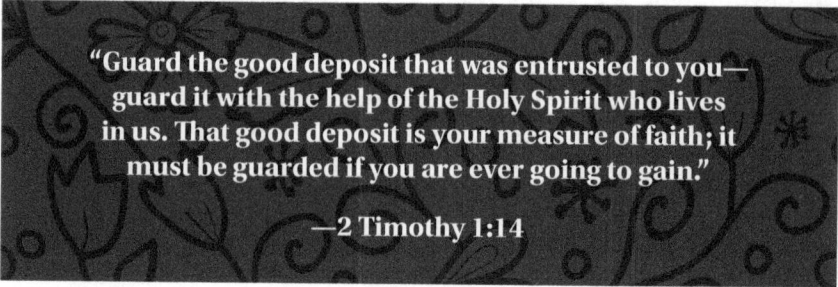

_____

_____

_____

_____

_____

_____

_____

_____

> "Guard the good deposit that was entrusted to you—
> guard it with the help of the Holy Spirit who lives
> in us. That good deposit is your measure of faith; it
> must be guarded if you are ever going to gain."
>
> —2 Timothy 1:14

Consider the scripture above and answer the following questions:

What does "guarding your measure of faith" mean, in your own words? In what ways are you guarding the faith that God has given you?

_____

_____

_____

_____

_____

_____

_____

Why does guarding result in gain? What are you gaining from guarding?

_____

_____

_____

_____

_____

_____

_____

_____

Consider the story of the servant who lost what was entrusted to him. What most stands out to you about this parable? What does it tell you about God's intimate knowledge of us? What does it tell you about how our knowledge of Him impacts our response to His instruction?

_____

_____

_____

_____

_____

_____

_____

The author identifies four roots of all excuses: fear of failure, fear of judgment, fear of change, and low self-esteem. Which of these do you find that you struggle with the most? How does it impede your willingness to bring God your increase?

_____

_____

_____

_____

_____

_____

_____

Reflect on a time when you experienced loss because you did not adequately guard something precious in your life. What was that experience like for you, and what did you learn from it?

_____

_____

_____

_____

_____

_____

_____

Consider the ways in which you are currently "gaining" in your spiritual life. How can you ensure that this gain is sustainable and aligned with God's will?

_____

_____

_____

_____

_____

_____

_____

How does the concept of stewardship play a role in your daily decisions and actions? What areas of your life require more intentional stewardship?

_____

_____

_____

_____

_____

_____

_____

HEART RHYTHM

You cannot pull out of others what is rooted in YOU.

READING TIME

As you read Chapter 7: "Heart Rhythm" in *Guarded*, review, reflect on, and respond to the text by answering the following questions.

REFLECT AND TAKE ACTION:

Reflect on the analogy of the treadmill as a tool for heart health. How are you doing with consistency and discipline to maintain a healthy heart rhythm?

_____

_____

_____

_____

_____

_____

_____

_____

_____

_____

Reflect on a time when your spiritual rhythm was disrupted. What caused the disruption, and how did you restore balance? What did you notice about the condition of your heart during this time?

_____

_____

_____

_____

_____

_____

_____

_____

_____

_____

What are some reasons why some people might struggle more than others with consistency and discipline, especially as it relates to the state of their reliance on and submission to God?

_____

_____

_____

_____

_____

_____

_____

_____

> *"If any of you lacks wisdom, you should ask God, who gives generously to all without finding fault, and it will be given to you. But when you ask, you must believe and not doubt, because the one who doubts is like a wave of the sea, blown and tossed by the wind. That person should not expect to receive anything from the Lord. Such a person is double-minded and unstable in all they do."*
>
> **—James 1:5-8 (NIV)**

Consider the scripture above and answer the following questions:

In what areas do you need wisdom right now? How confident are you in His willingness to provide it?

_____

_____

_____

_____

_____

The scripture warns against doubt and double-mindedness when you ask for wisdom. How has doubt affected your ability to receive direction from God in the past?

_____

_____

_____

_____

_____

_____

The author discusses the importance of creating a plan for optimal heart health, starting with your why. What is your goal?

_____

_____

_____

_____

_____

_____

Develop your own game plan for achieving your goal:

Daily: _____

_____

_____

_____

Weekly: _____

_____

_____

_____

Monthly: _____

_____

_____

_____

How closely do you follow the foundational goals in the chart for conditioning your spiritual ring? What new discipline could you begin to implement from each category?

_____

_____

_____

_____

_____

_____

_____

_____

_____

How closely do you follow the foundational goals in the chart for conditioning your emotional ring? What new discipline could you begin to implement from each category?

_____

_____

_____

_____

_____

_____

_____

_____

_____

How closely do you follow the foundational goals in the chart for conditioning your physical ring? What new discipline could you begin to implement from each category?

_____

_____

_____

_____

_____

_____

_____

_____

_____

CHAPTER 8

Shame-Free Zone

The Holy Spirit cannot overflow from
a heart bound by shame.

READING TIME

As you read Chapter 8: "Shame-Free Zone" in *Guarded*, review, reflect on, and respond to the text by answering the following questions.

REFLECT AND TAKE ACTION:

Jesus took our sins and shame upon Himself when He died on the cross. In light of this, what posture should we take when shame emerges from our hearts? Do you assume that posture?

_____

_____

_____

_____

_____

_____

_____

_____

_____

_____

Why does shame block the Holy Spirit from moving in and through our hearts?

_____

_____

_____

_____

_____

_____

_____

_____

_____

_____

How did Melissa and God work together to evict the shame of her past? How does this encourage you?

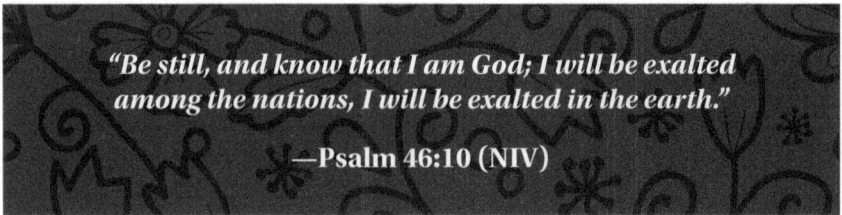

_____

_____

_____

_____

_____

_____

_____

_____

> *"Be still, and know that I am God; I will be exalted among the nations, I will be exalted in the earth."*
>
> **—Psalm 46:10 (NIV)**

Consider the scripture above and answer the following questions:

The phrase "be still" means "to move to a lower level." How can you seat yourself below Christ as you pray, read His Word, and worship?

_____

_____

_____

_____

_____

_____

_____

_____

How does your personal story communicate the glory of God to other people?

_____

_____

_____

_____

_____

_____

_____

How does shame subtly influence your thoughts and actions? What thoughts and actions do you believe are rooted in shame?

_____

_____

_____

_____

_____

_____

_____

Meditate on the statement, "He fills you to spill you." What does that mean, and are you allowing the Holy Spirit to fill you?

_____

_____

_____

_____

_____

_____

_____

_____

_____

What role does forgiveness play in maintaining a shame-free heart? Who do you need to forgive, or whose forgiveness do you need? How will you proceed to seek self-forgiveness and forgiveness of others?

_____

_____

_____

_____

_____

_____

_____

_____

_____

How do you balance accountability with the freedom from shame that Melissa describes? How can they coexist?

_____

_____

_____

_____

_____

_____

_____

_____

_____

Reflect on the idea of God's grace as a shame remover. Explain why it takes the grace of God to eliminate shame from your life.

_____

_____

_____

_____

_____

_____

_____

_____

_____

_____

MATTERS OF THE HEART

I guard what I treasure so that we don't treasure what we don't guard!

READING TIME

As you read Chapter 9: "Matters of the Heart" in *Guarded*, review, reflect on, and respond to the text by answering the following questions.

REFLECT AND TAKE ACTION:

Reflect on how you prioritize the matters of your heart. What takes precedence, should it take precedence, and how can you seek God's help in ordering the priorities of your heart to align with His?

_____

_____

_____

_____

_____

_____

_____

_____

_____

Who in your life is a journey person? A seasonal person? What tipped you off to this realization, and how has it served your efforts to guard your heart?

_____

_____

_____

_____

_____

_____

_____

_____

_____

How do you handle the pain of letting go of seasonal relationships while staying open to new ones?

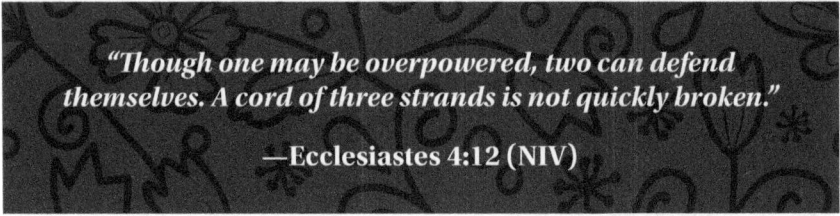

_____

_____

_____

_____

_____

_____

_____

_____

> *"Though one may be overpowered, two can defend themselves. A cord of three strands is not quickly broken."*
>
> **—Ecclesiastes 4:12 (NIV)**

Consider the scripture above and answer the following questions:

In this scripture, God represents the first cord, and we represent the second. Who represents the third cord in your life? What challenge(s) have you overcome with God and that person on your side?

_____

_____

_____

_____

_____

_____

_____

In what areas of your life are you currently trying to go it alone? What problems are emerging because of it, and how are they impacting your ability to be used by God?

_____

_____

_____

_____

_____

_____

In your own words, what is the difference between constructing walls and creating space? How high are your walls, and what kind of damage are they causing? What would it feel and look like to modify the heart space you give them instead?

_____

_____

_____

_____

_____

_____

_____

Reflect on the teacher's advice about not getting stuck on the season or timing but focusing on the purpose. How can you apply that wisdom to your current relationships?

_____

_____

_____

_____

_____

_____

_____

What is the most recent deep-seated issue in your heart that God has highlighted? What would it look like to allow the Holy Spirit to heal that issue?

_____

_____

_____

_____

_____

_____

_____

What relationships are shaping your heart? Do these relationships reflect two hearts rooted in Christ and not one another?

_____

_____

_____

_____

_____

_____

_____

_____

How comfortable are you with vulnerability? How transparent
are you with God? What holds you back from bringing your
mess to Him and inviting others to enter into your mess?

_____

_____

_____

_____

_____

_____

_____

What did you learn about guarding the hearts of your family
and children from the author's daughter's writing?

_____

_____

_____

_____

_____

_____

_____

LEADERS WHO FALL

*Success points to your fame, and
significance points to His.*

READING TIME

As you read
Chapter 10:
"Leaders
Who Fall"
in *Guarded*,
review,
reflect on,
and respond
to the text by
answering
the following
questions.

REFLECT AND TAKE ACTION:

Identify two prolific leaders—one who leads from the outflow of a servant's heart and one who leads from the outflow of a heart chasing success. What have you observed in each that influenced your choice?

_____

_____

_____

_____

_____

_____

_____

The author states that everyone is a leader. Did this statement surprise you? In what ways do you lead that challenge cultural ideas of conventional leadership?

_____

_____

_____

_____

_____

_____

_____

_____

_____

How do you respond to the failures of leaders in your life? What lessons have you learned from their mistakes?

_____

_____

_____

_____

_____

_____

_____

_____

> *"But each person is tempted when they are dragged away by their own evil desire and enticed. Then, after desire has conceived, it gives birth to sin; and sin, when it is full-grown, gives birth to death."*
>
> **—James 1:14-15 (NIV)**

Consider the scripture above and answer the following questions:

What does this scripture suggest about who is responsible for sin? In what areas of your life do you see the potential for progression from desire to sin?

_____

_____

_____

_____

_____

_____

According to this scripture, what is the danger of recurring desires of the flesh? How do you actively guard against being "dragged away" by your desires?

_____

_____

_____

_____

_____

_____

What kind of thoughts, beliefs, and actions indicate that a leader is dealing with unchecked humility? Describe the patterns you have observed in your own life.

_____

_____

_____

_____

_____

_____

_____

How does the fall of a leader impact the faith walks of others in the church? What happens to our hearts when we fall on our faces before Jesus?

_____

_____

_____

_____

_____

_____

_____

_____

Conduct an honest evaluation of why you lead. What intentions and goals are behind the reasons you lead?

_____

_____

_____

_____

_____

_____

_____

_____

In what ways is your leadership serving others and pointing them to Jesus? What is the evidence of this?

_____

_____

_____

_____

_____

_____

_____

_____

What are you doing now to equip the next generation of leaders?

_____

_____

_____

_____

_____

_____

_____

In what ways are you chasing success, and in what ways are you chasing significance? What adjustments can you make?

_____

_____

_____

_____

_____

_____

How does this book's emphasis on guarding your heart challenge your current lifestyle? What changes might you need to consider?

_____

_____

_____

_____

_____

_____

_____

_____

What are three big takeaways from this book that you intend to put into practice?

_____

_____

_____

_____

_____

_____

_____

_____

_____

guarded

Printed in the USA
CPSIA information can be obtained
at www.ICGtesting.com
CBHW021912291024
16595CB00008B/144

9 781962 401517